Stripes, Right?

By Deborah Schecter

A candy cane has stripes.
That is right!

Toothpaste has stripes.
That is right!

A flag has stripes.
That is right!

A zebra has stripes.
That is right!

A street has stripes.
That is right!

A ladybug has stripes.
That is NOT right!

It has spots!